Chemicals in Action

Atoms

Chris Oxlade

www.heinemann.co.uk/library
Visit our website to find out more information about **Heinemann Library** books.

To order:
 Phone 44 (0) 1865 888066
 Send a fax to 44 (0) 1865 314091
 Visit the Heinemann Bookshop at www.heinemann.co.uk/library to browse our catalogue and order online.

First published in Great Britain by Heinemann Library, Halley Court, Jordan Hill, Oxford OX2 8EJ, a division of Reed Educational and Professional Publishing Ltd. Heinemann is a registered trademark of Reed Educational & Professional Publishing Limited.

OXFORD MELBOURNE AUCKLAND JOHANNESBURG BLANTYRE
GABORONE IBADAN PORTSMOUTH NH (USA) CHICAGO

Designed by Tinstar Design (www.tinstar.co.uk)
Illustrations by Jeff Edwards.
Originated by Ambassador Litho Ltd.
Printed by Wing King Tong in Hong Kong.

ISBN 0 431 136009
06 05 04 03 02
10 9 8 7 6 5 4 3 2 1

British Library Cataloguing in Publication Data
Oxlade, Chris
        Atoms. – (Chemicals in action)
        1.Atoms – Juvenile literature
        I. Title
        539.7

Acknowledgements
The Publishers would like to thank the following for permission to reproduce photographs:

Ace Photo Agency pp12, 18, Andrew Lambert pp24, 33 (top), Bridgeman Art Library p9, Food Features p34, Mary Evans Picture Library pp8, 21, Milepost 92 p32, Oxford Scientific Films (David Macdonald) p35, Science Photo Library pp4, 5, 6, 7, 10, 11, 16, 19, 22, 25, 26, 36, 37, 38, 39, Trevor Clifford pp17, 23, 27, 29, 30, 31, 33 (bottom).

Cover photograph reproduced with permission of Science Photo Library (Mehau Kulyk).

The Publishers would like to thank Dr Nigel Saunders for his assistance in the preparation of this book.

Every effort has been made to contact copyright holders of any material reproduced in this book. Any omissions will be rectified in subsequent printings if notice is given to the Publisher.

Contents

Words appearing in the text in bold, **like this**, are explained in the glossary.

Chemicals in action

What's the link between plastics, the **genes** that control our bodies, and even nuclear weapons? The answer is **atoms**. They are all made of atoms or use atoms to work. In fact, almost every substance is made of atoms. Our knowledge of how atoms and other **particles** behave is used in making chemicals, in medical research, in power generation and engineering.

The study of atoms is part of the science of chemistry. Many people think of chemistry as something that scientists study by doing experiments in labs full of test tubes and flasks of bubbling liquids. This part of chemistry is very important. It is how scientists find out what substances are made of and how they make new materials – but this is only a tiny part of chemistry. Most chemistry happens away from laboratories, in factories and chemical plants. It is used to manufacture an enormous range of items, such as synthetic fibres for fabrics, drugs to treat diseases, explosives for fireworks, solvents for paints, and fertilizers for growing crops.

This is what happens when atoms split apart. A nuclear bomb test explosion on a Pacific atoll.

About the experiments and activities

There are several experiments and activities in the book for you to try. Doing these will help you to understand some of the chemistry in the book. An experiment is designed to help solve a scientific problem. Scientists use a logical approach to experiments so that they can conclude things from the results of the experiments. A scientist first writes down a hypothesis, which he or she thinks might be the answer to the problem, then designs an experiment to test the hypothesis. He or she then writes down the results of the experiment and concludes whether the results show that hypothesis is true or not. We only know what we do about chemistry because scientists have carefully carried out thousands of experiments over hundreds of years. Experiments have allowed scientists to discover that atoms exist, what they are made of, and how they join together.

Doing the experiments and activities

All the experiments and activities in this book have been designed for you to do at home with everyday substances and equipment. They can also be done in the school laboratory. Always follow the safety advice given with each experiment or activity, and ask an adult to help you when the instructions tell you to.

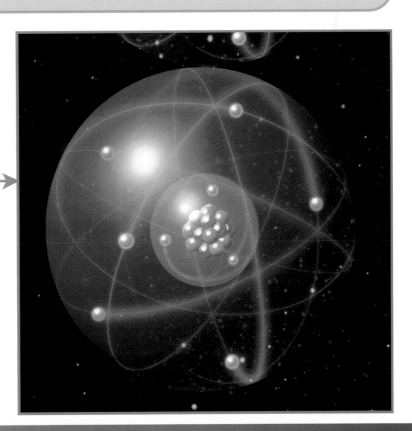

A model of an atom, made up of a nucleus with electrons around it. The actual atom is billions of times smaller.

All about atoms

Everything in your home or school (including you), everything on Earth, the Earth itself, and everything else in the whole Universe, is made of **matter**. When scientists use the word 'matter', they mean any substance that exists, from everyday substances such as wood, plastic, water and the air that we breathe, to the stars and planets deep in space.

All matter is made up of extremely tiny **particles** called **atoms**. Imagine breaking up an object, such as a **metal** drawing pin, into smaller and smaller pieces. If you kept breaking it up, eventually you would end up with just atoms of the metal, which you could not break up. Of course, this would be impossible in practice using everyday tools because the pieces of metal would soon become far too small to break.

Almost everything in the Universe, such as this enormous nebula (cloud of dust) and the stars that are being born in it, is made of atoms.

The size of atoms

Atoms are almost unimaginably small – even the biggest ones are less than a millionth of a millimetre across. If you were to write a full stop with a pencil, the full stop would contain millions of millions of carbon atoms from the graphite in the pencil. It also means that if you blew up those atoms until they were each a millimetre across, the full stop would become more than a kilometre wide!

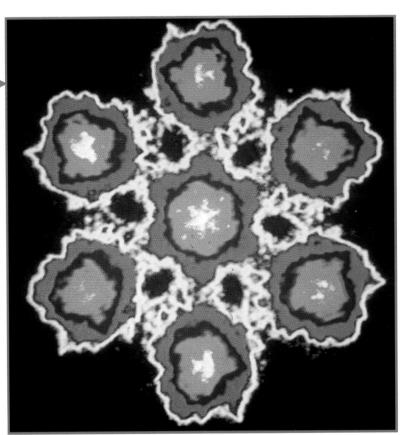

This tiny crystal, called a microcrystal, is made up of seven uranium atoms. The picture was taken with a scanning transmission electron microscope (STEM), which can magnify objects more than 90 million times.

Types of atom

There are many different types of atom, and 92 different types have been found naturally occurring on Earth. They make up the rocks and soil in the Earth's crust, the gases in the Earth's **atmosphere**, and the plants and animals that live on the Earth. More types of atoms have been made by scientists in laboratories, often by smashing other atoms together at extremely high speed. Very special conditions are needed to create these atoms, and the atoms normally only exist for a fraction of a second before they disintegrate again.

Different substances look different and have different **properties**, such as different strengths and **boiling points**. This is because they are made up of different types of atoms joined together in different ways.

Theories about matter

Some of the first people who tried to explain the **properties** and behaviour of **matter** were philosophers who lived in ancient Greece about two and a half thousand years ago. Their **theories** were really just guesses, often based on their religious beliefs, and they did not carry out experiments to test these theories. The philosophers were called 'natural philosophers'. One of the most famous was called Thales of Miletus, who lived in the 6th century BC. His theory was that all matter is made up of water.

Ideas about atoms

In 430BC another philosopher, Democritus of Abdera, tried to explain why different substances have different properties (such as different strengths, colours and tastes). His theory was that all

Greek philosopher Democritus of Abdera

matter is made up of tiny building blocks, and that these blocks cannot be divided into smaller pieces. He named the blocks 'atomos', which means 'indivisible'. This was the origin of the word atom that we use today. Democritus believed that in light substances, the blocks have big spaces between them, and that in heavy substances, the blocks are tightly packed together. He also believed that the properties of a substance are caused by the shape of the atoms in them. For example, he thought that things that tasted sour were made up of blocks with spikes on the outside!

Other Greek philosophers said that these ideas about atoms were nonsense. They agreed with another theory, that all matter was made from four basic elements – earth, fire, water and air. This theory said that different substances contained different amounts of the four elements.

Eventually most philosophers accepted the idea about four basic elements because two very important philosophers of the time, Aristotle and Plato, supported it. It is important to know that these philosophers did not do any experiments to test if their ideas were right or wrong. Their ideas were simply ideas, but they were still accepted two thousand years later, in the 17th century.

Gold from lead

The chemists of the Middle Ages (which lasted from about the 5th century AD to about the 15th century AD) were called alchemists. Alchemy was a strange mixture of science, magic, astrology and religion. One of the things alchemists tried to do was to make gold and silver from other metals, such as lead and mercury. They did not succeed, but they did discover many new substances in the process.

'The Alchemist's Workshop', painted in 1570, shows alchemists at work trying to make precious metals from everyday metals.

Experimental science

The earth, air, fire and water idea of the Greek philosophers was accepted as the truth in Europe for many centuries. Things only began to change after the 15th century, when scientists started to carry out proper scientific experiments.

One of the most important things that scientists needed to do was to find out what **matter** was made of. Gradually the scientists realized that the ancient Greek idea about the four elements was incorrect. Instead, the idea that matter is made of **atoms** became accepted by most scientists. Amongst them was Irishman Robert Boyle (1627–91), who defined a thing called an **element**. He said that an element was a substance made up of atoms that cannot be broken into more simple substances. He also suggested that most substances are not elements, but are made up of different elements combined together, and said that atoms come in different shapes and sizes.

Robert Boyle (1627–1691) was one of the first scientists to do experiments in a logical way. He argued that chemists should not be trying to turn lead into gold, but should be working out what substances are made from.

Because these scientists used experiments to try to prove their **theories**, their work became known as experimental science. There was a fast expansion in experimental science in the 18th and 19th centuries. The knowledge we have today about atoms and how they combine to make different substances was gradually discovered during this time.

Dalton's atomic theory

One of the most important theories, called the **atomic theory**, came from John Dalton (see below). He decided that there are a limited number of types of atom, which combine together to form millions of different substances. Dalton stated that each element (such as carbon, oxygen or iron) is made up of atoms; that all the atoms of an element are the same; and that atoms cannot be broken apart. Before this, many scientists believed that each and every different substance was made up of a different type of atom.

John Dalton (1766–1844)

English scientist John Dalton lived in northern England and spent most of his life in Manchester. He was very intelligent and started working as a teacher at his local school when he was just twelve years old! He became a full-time scientist in his mid-thirties. As well as chemistry, he studied colour-blindness (from which he suffered) and the weather, which he recorded on nearly every day of his life. Some of Dalton's ideas were wrong and some of his experiments inaccurate, but his atomic theory became the basis of modern theories about matter.

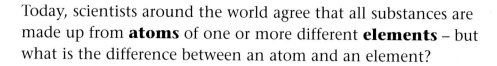

Atoms and elements

Today, scientists around the world agree that all substances are made up from **atoms** of one or more different **elements** – but what is the difference between an atom and an element?

An atom is an extremely tiny **particle** of **matter**, and there are more than a hundred different types of atom. An element is a substance that contains only one type of atom. For example, iron is an element, it is made up just of iron atoms. Every atom in a piece of iron is exactly the same as all the others. Because an element is made up of just one type of atom, there is an element for each different type of atom. So there are the same number of elements as there are different types of atoms.

Metals and non-metals

About three-quarters of the elements are **metals**, such as iron, aluminium, copper, silver and gold. Metals are shiny, they are good **conductors** of heat and electricity, and they are solid at room temperature. The only exception is mercury, which is a liquid metal.

The rest of the elements are **non-metals**, such as carbon, oxygen, hydrogen, nitrogen and sulfur. Most non-metals are poor conductors of heat and electricity. Most are gases at room temperature, a few are solids and only one, bromine, is a liquid.

Some elements are called **metalloids** or semi-metals. This is because they have some of the **properties** of metals, and some of the properties of non-metals.

Spectacular metal cladding on the Guggenheim Museum, Spain.

Names and symbols

Every element has a name, and scientists have also given each element a **symbol** that is used to represent the element in **chemical formulae** and equations. Each symbol is an abbreviation (a shortened version) of the element's name. For example, the chemical symbol for the element carbon is C. The symbols of elements do not always seem to match the elements' names – this is because the symbols come from different languages. For example, the symbol for iron is Fe, which comes from 'ferro', the Greek word for iron.

Compounds and mixtures

All substances are either elements, **compounds** or **mixtures**. An element is made up of only one type of atom. Carbon and oxygen are both elements. A compound is a substance made up of two or more elements joined together. For example, when carbon atoms join to oxygen atoms, they make carbon dioxide, which is a compound. If carbon atoms are just mixed with oxygen atoms, and are not joined to them, you get a mixture. A mixture can also contain compounds, as long as they are not joined to the other substances in the mixture. For example, air is a mixture of elements such as nitrogen and oxygen, and compounds such as water and carbon dioxide.

This diagram shows the difference between two separate elements, a simple compound made up of the elements joined together, and a mixture of the two elements.

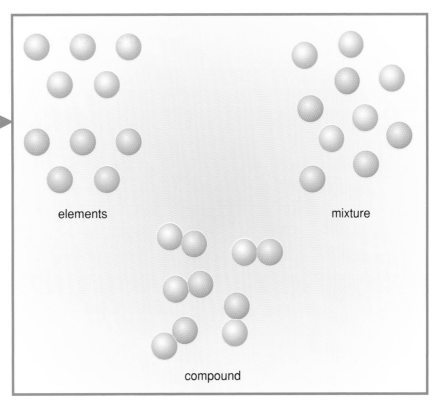

elements

mixture

compound

Inside atoms

Atoms themselves are extremely tiny, but they are made up of even tinier **particles**. These particles are impossible to see even with the most powerful microscopes, but they can be detected with sensitive scientific instruments. They are called **sub-atomic particles** because they are even smaller than an atom.

The nucleus

At the centre of every atom is a **nucleus**. The nucleus is made up of particles called **protons** and **neutrons**, joined closely to each other in a bunch.

In most atoms there are about the same number of protons and neutrons in the nucleus. For example, the nucleus of a carbon atom contains six protons and six neutrons, and the nucleus of a lithium atom contains three protons and four neutrons. The simplest atoms are hydrogen atoms, because the nucleus is a single proton.

The nucleus of an atom is extremely small compared to the size of the atom itself. Imagine if an atom was blown up to the size of an Olympic running track, its nucleus would still only be the size of a garden pea!

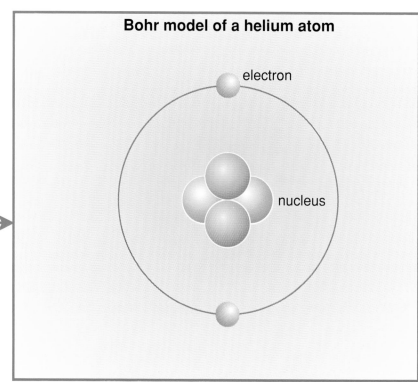

At the centre of every atom is a nucleus, made up of protons and neutrons. Electrons whiz around the nucleus.

The protons and neutrons in the nucleus of an atom make up nearly all its weight, and protons and neutrons weigh the same as each other. Protons also have a tiny electric **charge**. This charge is the same sort of thing as you get on your hair when you comb it and it stands up on its own. There are two types of electric charge – positive and negative. Protons have a positive electric charge, neutrons have no electric charge.

Electrons

Whizzing around the nucleus are particles called **electrons**. They are a fraction of the size and weight of protons and neutrons. In a complete atom, there is always the same number of electrons as there are protons in the nucleus. Electrons have a negative electric charge, equal in size but opposite to the charge on a proton. In a complete atom the negative charges of the electrons cancel out the positive charges of the protons, so overall there is no electric charge.

Atomic number and mass

The atoms of different **elements** have different numbers of protons, neutrons and electrons. All the atoms of an element have the same number of protons. For example, all carbon atoms have six protons. The number of protons in an atom is called its atomic number, sometimes called its proton number. The atomic number of carbon is six, because its atoms all have six protons. If you add the number of protons in an atom to the number of neutrons in an atom, you get the atom's mass number. The mass number of a carbon atom with six protons and six neutrons is twelve.

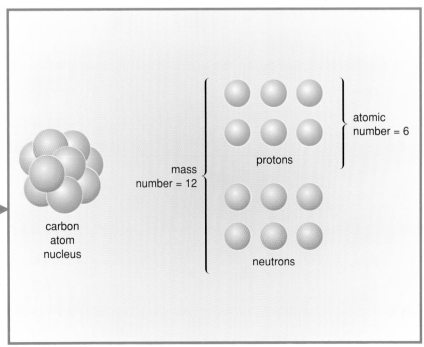

This diagram shows how the number of protons and neutrons in an atom of carbon relate to its mass number and atomic number.

carbon atom nucleus

mass number = 12

protons

atomic number = 6

neutrons

Model atoms

You often see diagrams similar to the one on page 14 that shows what an **atom** looks like, but atoms don't actually look like this! The drawings only show what scientists think the structure of an atom is like – they are models of atoms. Scientists have never actually seen an atom because the **sub-atomic particles** are invisible. They only have evidence from experiments about what the structure is like, so the models are really still **theories**.

Scientists know that atoms have a **nucleus** at the centre, and **electrons** around them, but don't really know how the electrons move around the nucleus. In some atomic models, electrons are shown orbiting the nucleus, like the planets orbiting the Sun, and in other models they are shown moving about in groups.

Developing a model atom

The modern model of the atom was developed by British physicist Ernest Rutherford (1871–1937) and Danish physicist Niels Bohr (1885–1962). In 1911 Rutherford carried out an experiment in which he fired sub-atomic particles at a sheet of material. He found that most went straight through but a few bounced back. He concluded that atoms must be made up mostly of empty space, with their mass concentrated in a central nucleus. Most **particles** simply went straight through the empty spaces and only a few hit the nuclei and bounced back. In 1913 Bohr (seen here) developed his atomic model that shows electrons orbiting the nucleus in different layers called **shells**.

Activity: Making models of atoms

Here you can see how to make some simple models of atoms. They will help you to understand and remember the structure of atoms.

EQUIPMENT
modelling clay in three different colours

Activity steps

1 Make six balls about 10mm across from one colour of modelling clay. These are your model **protons**.

Make six more balls the same size, but in a different colour. These are your model **neutrons**.

Make six balls about 5mm across, but in a third colour. These are your model electrons.

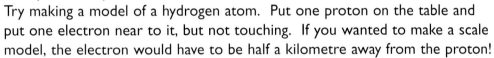

2 Hydrogen is the simplest atom. It only has one proton and one electron. Try making a model of a hydrogen atom. Put one proton on the table and put one electron near to it, but not touching. If you wanted to make a scale model, the electron would have to be half a kilometre away from the proton!

3 Try making a model helium atom. Make a nucleus by joining two protons and two neutrons into a bunch, and put two electrons in an imaginary circle around it. Remember not to let the electrons touch the nucleus or each other.

4 Try making a model carbon atom (carbon atoms have six protons, six neutrons and six electrons). When you put the electrons around the nucleus, put two electrons close to the nucleus and the other four electrons further away. This models two electron shells.

5 The number of protons is called the atomic number. What is the atomic number of carbon?

The number of protons added to the number of neutrons is called the mass number. What is the mass number of carbon?

6 The proton number of beryllium is four and its mass number is nine. Try making a model beryllium atom.

Joining atoms

Objects like this book, your pen, and your whole body are made up of countless billions of **atoms**. These atoms must be joined together otherwise the objects would fall apart, but exactly how are atoms joined to each other? The answer is that they are joined together by links called **chemical bonds**.

Making atoms stable

As we have seen, **electrons** are arranged around the **nucleus** of an atom in layers called **shells**. The shells are like the layers of skin on an onion. Each layer can hold a certain number of electrons before it becomes full. When it is full, another layer is started, and the more electrons an atom has, the more shells it needs to hold them all.

Stable or unreactive atoms have completely full outer shells. If an atom has an outer shell with only one or two electrons, it is unstable and **reactive**. It can become stable by losing its outer electrons. This empties the shell, and leaves the full shell underneath as the new outer shell. An atom is also unstable if it needs one or two electrons to fill its outer shell. In this case, it can become stable by gaining electrons from another atom to fill its outer shell. It can also become stable by sharing electrons with another atom.

Atoms that have only one or two electrons in their outer shell often give them away to become stable. For example, a sodium atom has only one electron in its outer shell. It always loses this electron to become stable. This leaves it with eleven positively **charged** protons but only ten negatively charged electrons, so overall it has a single positive charge. The sodium atom has become a sodium **ion**, and its symbol is Na$^+$.

All the noble gases are unreactive. This airship is full of helium, which would not explode in an accident.

*Metallic bonds are generally very strong, which is why metals tend to have very high **melting points**. This metal has been heated so that it can be rolled into sheets.*

Atoms that need one or two electrons to give them a full outer shell often gain extra electrons from other atoms to become stable. For example, a chlorine atom has an outer shell that needs one more electron to make it full. So, a chlorine atom will gain one electron to become stable. This leaves it with seventeen positively charged protons but eighteen negatively charged electrons, so overall it has a single negative charge. The chlorine atom has become a chloride ion, and its symbol is Cl^-.

Atoms that have too few electrons to make a full shell can become stable by sharing electrons with each other. Two atoms can become so close together that they can share the electrons in their outer shells. If two electrons are shared, this makes a bond between the two atoms called a **covalent bond**. For example, a chlorine atom has seventeen electrons, but needs eighteen to have a full outer shell. If two chlorine atoms join together so that they share two electrons, both of them will have eighteen electrons. They will be joined together by a covalent bond, and both atoms will be stable.

Metallic bonding

In a piece of **metal**, such as iron, the atoms become stable by sharing electrons. In metals, the electrons that are shared are not fixed in their shells, they can move from atom to atom. This does not make the atoms unstable, because overall each atom still has enough electrons. An electric current is made up of a stream of electrons, so metals are good **conductors** of electricity.

The periodic table

The periodic table is a list of all the known **elements**, arranged in order of the atomic numbers of their **atoms**, starting at the top left and working across and down. Elements with similar **properties** to each other are close together. For example, fluorine (F) is a gas that reacts very easily with other elements and so is chlorine (Cl). The periodic table gets its name from the fact that the properties the elements have repeat themselves every few elements, or periodically. A chemist can tell what the properties of an element are likely to be by looking at its position in the table.

Groups and periods

The vertical columns of elements are called groups. Elements in a group all have similar properties to each other. The horizontal rows of elements are called periods. The table also shows which elements are **metals**, which are **non-metals** and which are **metalloids**. Some groups have special names:

Group 1: The alkali metals
Group 2: The alkaline earth metals
Group 7: The halogens
Group 0: The noble gases

The periodic table, showing the position of each group (vertical block of elements). A full table is on page 40.

Group 1	Group 2					
H						
Li	Be					
Na	Mg					
K	Ca					
Rb	Sr				Transition metals	
Cs	Ba					
Fr	Ra					

Dmitri Mendeleyev (1834–1907)

The Russian scientist Dmitri Mendeleyev was born in Siberia and became a chemistry professor at St Petersburg in 1866. In 1869 he drew up the first periodic table. Mendeleyev's clever idea was to leave spaces in the table where no elements fitted neatly. He predicted that elements would soon be discovered to fill the gaps, and by 1950 they all had!

		Group 3	Group 4	Group 5	Group 6	Group 7	Group 0
							He
		B	C	N	O	F	Ne
		Al	Si	P	S	Cl	Ar
		Ga	Ge	As	Se	Br	Kr
		In	Sn	Sb	Te	I	Xe
		Tl	Pb	Bi	Po	At	Rn
			Uuq				

Molecules

All substances are made up of tiny **particles** of some sort. In some substances, the particles are individual **atoms** or **ions**, and in other substances, they are groups of atoms called **molecules**. A molecule is made up of two or more atoms joined together by **covalent bonds**. For example, a hydrogen molecule is made up of two hydrogen atoms joined together by one covalent bond; an oxygen molecule is made up of two oxygen atoms joined together by two covalent bonds.

A **compound** is a substance that contains two or more different **elements**. Many compounds are made up of molecules. For example, water is a compound of oxygen and hydrogen that is made up of molecules. Each and every water molecule contains one oxygen atom and two hydrogen atoms.

Symbols and formulae

Scientists need a clear way of showing what atoms are in the molecules of a substance, and they do this using **chemical formulae**. The formula tells you how many atoms of each element are in each of its molecules. For example, the formula of oxygen is O_2, which shows that each oxygen molecule contains two oxygen atoms. The formula for water is H_2O, which shows that each water molecule contains two atoms of hydrogen and one atom of oxygen.

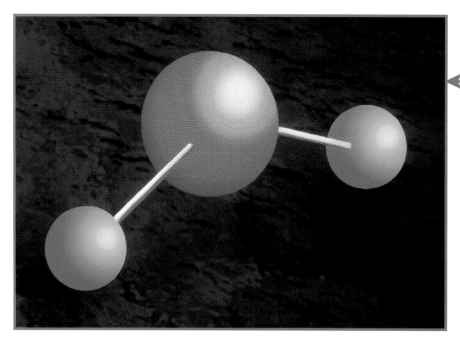

A model of a molecule of water. Each and every water molecule has an oxygen atom with two hydrogen atoms joined to it.

Experiment: Making molecules

PROBLEM: How do molecules of compounds form?

HYPOTHESIS: Molecules of a compound contain atoms of different elements, and they could be formed when molecules of the elements react together.

EQUIPMENT
modelling clay (two different colours)
matchsticks or wooden dowels

Experiment steps

1 Make four balls about 10mm across from one colour of modelling clay. These are your model hydrogen atoms. Make two balls about 20mm across and in a different colour. These are your model oxygen atoms.

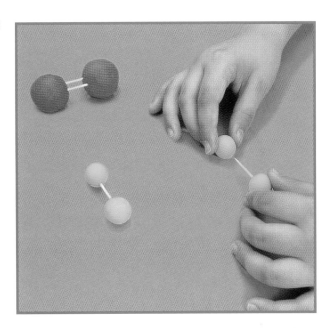

2 Make a model hydrogen molecule by joining two hydrogen atoms together with a matchstick. Make sure the atoms do not touch each other. The matchstick is the model bond between the two hydrogen atoms. Make one more hydrogen molecule.

3 Make a model oxygen molecule by joining two oxygen atoms using two matchsticks side by side (oxygen atoms can make two bonds each).

4 Now model the reaction between hydrogen and oxygen to make water. Take apart the model hydrogen molecules and oxygen molecule and join them up to make two water molecules (each water molecule is made of two hydrogen atoms joined to an oxygen atom). If you have done it correctly, you will still have the same number of atoms and bonds as you started with.

This is the symbol equation for the reaction:

$$2H_2 \; + \; O_2 \longrightarrow 2H_2O$$

Simple molecules and giant molecules

The **molecules** of many substances, such as oxygen and water, are made up of a small number of **atoms**. Molecules like this are called simple molecules. The molecules of other substances are made up of hundreds or even thousands of atoms. These really big molecules are called giant molecules or macromolecules.

Organic molecules

Many **compounds** with huge, complex molecules, such as proteins, are found in the cells of animals and plants. They are called **organic compounds**. All organic compounds contain the **element** carbon. Carbon atoms can form four bonds. They join with each other to form long chains, often with branches, and sometimes complete rings of atoms. Organic compounds are also found in crude oil, gas and coal because these were formed from the remains of animals and plants.

Polymers

A **polymer** is an organic compound with extremely long chains made up of thousands of carbon atoms. Polymers are made by joining hundreds or thousands of smaller molecules (called monomers) together. This process is called polymerization.

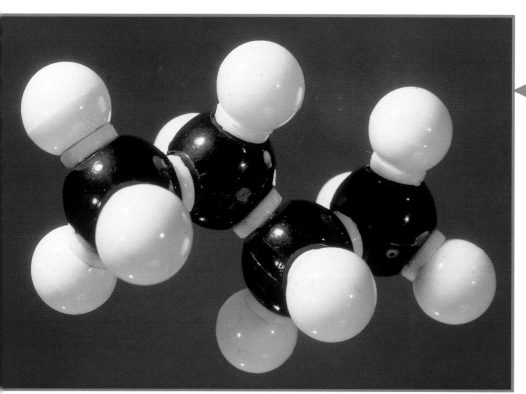

A model of a molecule of butane (C_4H_{10}). Butane is an organic compound with a chain of four carbon atoms.

All plastics are polymers, for example, the plastic polythene. Polythene is used to make items such as plastic sheets and washing-up bowls and is made by joining up ethene molecules.

The amazing buckyball

Some organic compounds have molecules that are like cages of carbon atoms. These molecules are called fullerenes, and they can be shaped like balls or cylinders. One of the first to be discovered was made up of 60 carbon atoms, and it was called buckminsterfullerene (nicknamed the buckyball) after the American architect Buckminster Fuller. He invented a similar-shaped dome for buildings. In the future, buckyballs may be used as tiny ball bearings in microscopic machines called nanomachines, for making drugs, and in electronic circuits.

Discovering DNA

The chemical **DNA** is present in every cell of animals and plants, and it contains the **genes** that pass **genetic information** from one generation to the next. A molecule of DNA is very complicated, it contains more than a billion atoms. At the beginning of the 1950s scientists knew that DNA existed but they did not know the structure of its molecule. In 1951 the British scientist Rosalind Franklin (1920–58) analysed DNA using a technique called **X-ray** crystallography. This showed that DNA has a structure like a twisted ladder. British scientist Francis Crick and American scientist James Watson used this information to help them build a model of DNA. This was one of the most important steps in the development of the science of genetics. By the way, DNA is short for deoxyribonucleic acid!

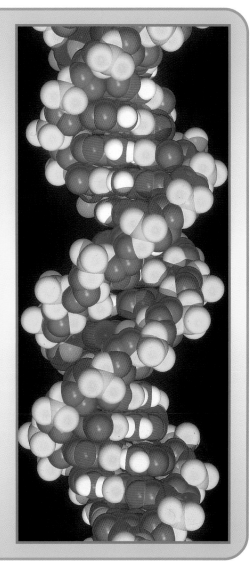

Forming solids

Substances come in three different forms or states – solids, liquids and gases. A solid is a substance that keeps its shape, it does not flow like a gas or a liquid. Most **elements** and **compounds** are solids at room temperature. Inside solids the **particles** (which are either **atoms, ions** or **molecules**) are packed tightly together and joined to their neighbours – but what holds a solid together? The answer is the bonds between the particles that make it up.

Different properties

Many of the **properties** of a substance, such as its strength and its **melting** and **boiling points**, depend on how its particles are arranged and what sort of bond joins them together.

If the bonds between the particles in a substance are very strong, the substance will have a high melting point and boiling point. This means that it will be a solid at room temperature. For example, sodium chloride (common salt) melts at 801°C, so it is a solid at room temperature. It is made of sodium ions and chloride ions joined together by **ionic bonds**. Ionic bonds are very strong, so **ionic compounds** like sodium chloride have very high melting points and boiling points. Giant molecules are also solids at room temperature. For example, diamond melts at over 3550°C! In diamond, each carbon atom is joined to four other carbon atoms by **covalent bonds**. Covalent bonds are very strong, and diamond has lots of them, so it has a very high melting point and boiling point.

If the bonds between the particles in a substance are weak, the substance will have a low melting point and boiling point. This means that it will be a liquid or a gas at room temperature. For example, at room temperature, water is a liquid and carbon dioxide is a gas. This is because they are made of simple molecules. There are strong covalent bonds between the atoms in a simple molecule, but the bonds between the molecules are weak and easily broken.

The particles in quartz crystals have strong bonds between them.

Experiment: Diamond and graphite

PROBLEM: Diamond and graphite are two forms of the same element – carbon. Why are their properties so different?

HYPOTHESIS: Carbon and graphite are both made up of only carbon atoms. The differences between them may be because the carbon atoms are joined in different arrangements.

EQUIPMENT
modelling clay
matchsticks or
wooden dowels

Experiment steps

1 Make 20 balls about 10mm across from modelling clay, these are model carbon atoms.

2 Make a model of a piece of diamond like the one shown in this picture (right). Each carbon atom is attached to four others around it to make a three-dimensional structure.

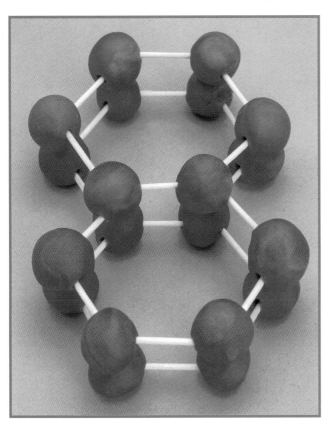

3 Make a model of a piece of graphite as shown (left). Each carbon atom is attached to three others like a honeycomb to make sheets. Each sheet is loosely attached to one sheet above and one below.

CONCLUSION: You can see that the structure of diamond is very strong because the atoms cannot move about in the structure. Graphite is made up of sheets of carbon atoms which can slide past each other, so it is not as strong.

The particle model

We can explain many of the **properties** and behaviour of substances by thinking of them as being made up of tiny **particles** that are **atoms**, **ions** or **molecules**. This model of substances is known as the particle model. The particle model helps to explain the differences between solids, liquids and gases and what happens during melting and boiling.

Solids, liquids and gases

The particles in solids, liquids and gases are arranged differently and can move differently. In solids, the particles are close together and arranged neatly in a regular pattern. The bonds between the particles hold them tightly in place, so the particles in a solid can only vibrate where they are. They cannot move about or change places with their neighbours. This means that solids keep their shape and cannot flow.

In liquids, the particles are close together, but they are not arranged neatly in a regular pattern. The bonds between the particles hold them tightly, but they can break and then form again. This allows the particles in a liquid to move around each other. This means that liquids can flow into the bottom of any container they are in.

In gases, the particles are widely spaced, and they are not arranged neatly in a regular pattern. There are no bonds between the particles, so the particles can zoom about randomly at high speed. This means that gases can flow to completely fill any container they are in.

Solids cannot flow, because there are strong bonds between the particles. A liquid flows to the bottom of a container, while a gas flows to fill it.

solid   liquid   gas

Experiment: Particles in solids, liquids and gases

PROBLEM: Why do solids, liquids and gases flow differently?

HYPOTHESIS: Solids, liquids and gases flow differently because of how the particles that make them up are joined. We can use model particles to test this.

EQUIPMENT
modelling clay
glass jar with lid

Experiment steps

1 Use the modelling clay to make twelve to fifteen small balls, each about 10mm across, and place them in a glass jar. Put the lid on.

2 Tip and roll the jar gently in your hand (below) and watch what happens to the balls.

3 Now shake the jar as you roll it about and watch what happens.

4 Finally, shake the jar really hard and watch what happens.

CONCLUSION: In step 2 the balls stick to each other, they do not flow at all, but make a solid. In step 3 the balls stick a bit, but flow into the bottom of the jar, and make a liquid. In step 4 the balls do not stick at all, they flow all over the jar. They make a gas.

Gas pressure

When a gas is put into a container, the **particles** of gas zoom about hitting each other and the sides of the container. The particles of gas are very small because they are usually single **atoms** or simple **molecules**. However, there are millions upon millions of them in a cupful of gas, so lots of them are hitting the inside of the container all the time. This means that the gas particles push against the surface of the container, and this 'push' is called gas pressure.

Diffusion

When different liquids or gases are put into the same container, they gradually mix even if they are not stirred. This mixing is called **diffusion**. Diffusion happens because the particles in liquids and gases can move about, and so they gradually spread into each other. This is how smells reach your nose through the air, even when there is no breeze blowing. For example, if a bottle of perfume is opened, particles from the perfume move quickly, mixing with the particles in the air, and reaching your nose by diffusion.

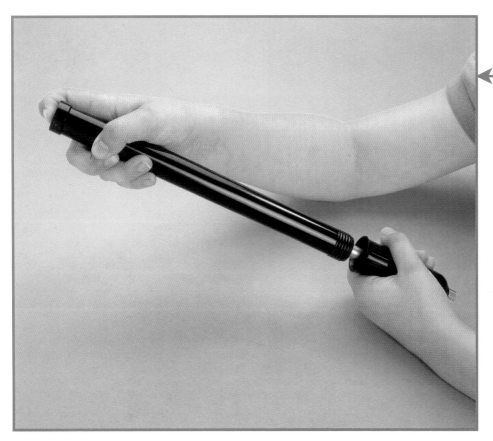

When you squeeze the air in a bicycle pump the air molecules inside are pushed together, making the pressure go up. They hit the end of the piston more often, pushing it outwards.

Experiment: Diffusion of liquids

PROBLEM: How can we show that diffusion happens in liquids?

HYPOTHESIS: By putting coloured liquids next to each other, we can see if they mix together without any mechanical mixing.

EQUIPMENT
two identical glass jars
kitchen foil
Vaseline or grease
food colouring

Experiment steps

1 Smear the rim of one of the jars with Vaseline, then fill the jar to the brim with warm water. Add a few drops of food colouring to the water.

2 Cut a piece of kitchen foil that will fit over the mouth of the jar, and smooth the foil over the mouth and down over the neck. It does not matter if some air is trapped under the foil.

3 Do these next steps over a sink or basin in case it goes wrong! Smear the rim of the other jar with Vaseline and fill to the brim with warm water. Overfill so that the jar is really brimming full. Take the jar with the coloured water and turn it upside down over the jar with the colourless water.

4 Wait a few minutes for the water to settle. You might need a helper to hold the bottom jar firmly. Hold onto the top jar and very slowly pull the foil out. You must keep the rims of the two jars exactly together while you do this. Watch what happens over the next few minutes.

CONCLUSION: Even though the water is not stirred, the colour spreads from one jar to the other. This shows that the particles of water from both jars are diffusing into each other.

Heating and cooling

The **particle** theory helps to explain what happens to substances when they are heated up or cooled down. It explains why substances expand (get bigger) when they are heated, and why they melt or boil. It also explains why substances contract (get smaller) when they are cooled down, and why they freeze or **condense**.

Expansion and contraction

In a solid the particles cannot move about because they are joined tightly to each other, but they can vibrate about where they are. As a solid is heated up, its particles get more energy and they vibrate more and more, so the higher the temperature, the more the particles vibrate. The particles do not get bigger, but they do take up more space, and this makes the solid expand slightly. Liquids also expand as their particles move more quickly.

When a gas is heated up, its particles move faster and faster. This means that the particles hit the sides of the container that the gas is in faster and more often. So the pressure that the gas exerts on the container is greater. If there is no container, the gas expands to fill more space.

Metal rails expand in hot weather. Expansion joints allow this to happen, without the rails buckling.

Expanding metals

1 The apparatus (right) has two parts: a metal rod and holder. When the rod is cold it just fits inside the holder.

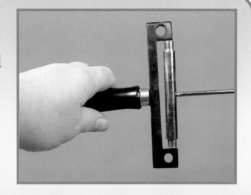

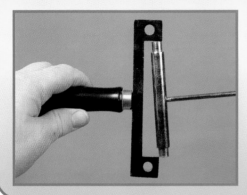

2 If the metal rod is heated by a Bunsen burner, it expands slightly and becomes too big to fit inside the holder.

Experiment: Expanding air

PROBLEM: How can we show that air expands when it is heated?

HYPOTHESIS: Gases expand much more than solids when they are heated. We can detect the air expanding and escaping from a bottle as it warms up.

EQUIPMENT
empty plastic bottle
small coin

I Wet a coin and rest it over the top of an empty plastic pop bottle. Put your hands around the bottle without squeezing it. Watch the coin carefully.

CONCLUSION: After a few seconds the coin flips up. The air in the bottle has expanded because of the heat from your hands.

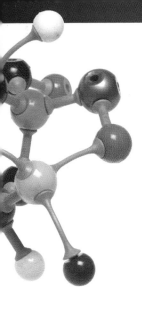

Temperature and heat

The **particle** model also helps to explain temperature and heat, and the difference between them. The temperature of an object is a measure of how hot it is, and the more the particles in an object are vibrating, the higher its temperature.

Heat is a form of energy, so when an object is heated each particle gets more energy and vibrates more, and the object's temperature goes up. Imagine you have two metal blocks one larger than the other, the larger block has more particles than the smaller block. If you add the same amount of heat to each block the smaller one will become hotter than the larger one. This is because each particle gets more energy and vibrates more.

Changes of state

The particle theory explains how substances change from solid to liquid, and from liquid to gas. These changes are called changes of state, and they happen when the **chemical bonds** between particles break. When a solid is heated up, its particles vibrate

more and more until some of the bonds between them break. This allows the particles to begin moving around each other, and the substance becomes a liquid. When a solid turns into a liquid, it is called melting.

In a pan of boiling water the particles, which are water molecules, are breaking away from each other to form a gas, which we call steam.

When a liquid is heated up, its particles move faster and faster. The bonds to some of the particles break completely and these particles can escape from the liquid to form a gas. When a liquid turns into a gas in this way, it is called boiling. Liquids can also turn into gases by evaporating. This happens when some particles in the liquid already have enough energy to escape to form a gas. Evaporating happens below the **boiling point** of the liquid.

The particle theory also explains how substances change from gas to liquid, and from liquid to solid. These changes of state happen when bonds between particles are made. When a gas is cooled down, its particles slow down until some bonds begin to form between the particles, and the particles join together to form a liquid. This is called **condensing**. When a liquid is cooled down, its particles slow down so much that lots of bonds form. The particles join up in a regular pattern. This is called freezing or solidifying.

Making solutions

A **solution** is made when a solid dissolves in a liquid. For example, if you put common salt in water, the salt crystals get smaller and seem to disappear as they dissolve. The particles on the outside of the crystal are pulled off by the water **molecules**, as the water molecules collide with the crystals, and then they **diffuse** through the water. The hotter the water, the faster the water molecules move and the faster the salt dissolves.

Sunshine has heated the water in this lake, making it evaporate into the air. Evaporation happens faster when the temperature is higher and the air is dry.

Splitting atoms

When **atoms** take part in chemical reactions they can lose some **electrons** or gain some electrons, but their **nuclei** stay in one piece. However, the nucleus of an atom can be split up, or extra **neutrons** and **protons** added to it. When this happens it is called a nuclear reaction because the nucleus changes.

Nuclear reactions can be both harmful and helpful. For example, the **radiation** they release can cause cancer, but in small doses radiation is actually used to kill cancer cells. Also, the energy the reactions release can create massively destructive explosions, but it is also used to produce electricity.

Radioactive elements

The atoms of some **elements**, such as uranium, have nuclei that contain hundreds of protons and neutrons. Nuclei this big are

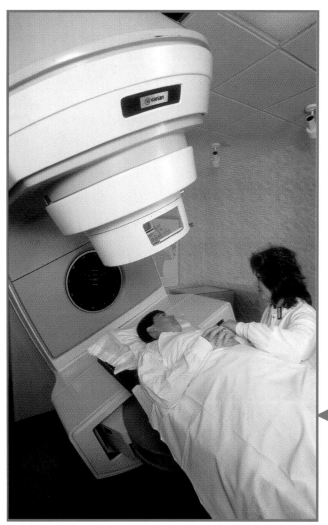

quite unstable and neutrons and protons often break away – making the nuclei smaller and more stable. This process is called radioactive **decay**, and the atoms that decay are described as **radioactive**. After a nuclear reaction, the nucleus of an atom often has fewer protons than it did before – so the atom is an atom of a different element.

Radiotherapy is the use of radiation in medicine to try to kill cancer cells.

Here's an example of a nuclear reaction. Uranium has an atomic number of 92, so all uranium atoms contain 92 protons. Some uranium atoms contain 146 neutrons, which means they have a mass number of 238. This form of uranium is called uranium-238. When the nucleus of a uranium-238 atom decays it loses a **particle** called an alpha particle, which is made up of two protons and two neutrons. This leaves the nucleus with 90 protons and 144 neutrons. The atom's atomic number has changed, so it is no longer an atom of uranium. It is now an atom of an element called thorium.

Radiation

When a nucleus breaks up it releases radiation. Radiation can be made up of particles, such as the alpha particles mentioned in the nuclear reaction above. Radiation can also be made up of rays. These rays are like light rays, but they are invisible and have so much more energy that they can go through solid sheets of **metal**. Strong radiation causes radiation sickness, which makes people feel sick and be sick. It can also cause burns to skin, and cancers. Radioactive substances are stored in lead-lined boxes that stop radiation getting out.

Natural radiation

Most rocks contain radioactive elements, so there is always a small, harmless, amount of natural radiation from the ground. This is called background radiation. All living things contain millions of carbon atoms, some of these atoms are called carbon-14 atoms because they contain two more neutrons than a normal carbon atom. These atoms decay naturally so even your body creates tiny amounts of radiation!

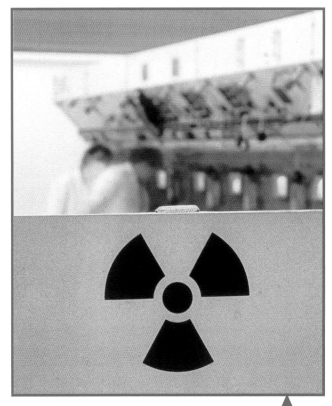

This hazard symbol warns that there are high levels of harmful radiation in this room.

Nuclear energy

In **radioactive decay**, **neutrons** and **protons** split from the **nucleus** of an **atom**, leaving a slightly smaller nucleus behind. Nuclei can also split in two, to make two smaller nuclei. This sort of nuclear reaction is also called **nuclear fission**. It means that an atom of one **element** becomes two atoms of different elements.

Nuclear fission happens naturally, but we can also make it happen deliberately by firing **sub-atomic particles** such as neutrons into a large nucleus. For example, when a neutron is fired into the nucleus of an atom of uranium-235, the atom splits up into an atom of an element called strontium and an atom of an element called xenon. Some neutrons are also released. If there are more atoms of uranium nearby, these neutrons make them split up too, and these release neutrons too, and so on. This is called a **chain reaction**. Nuclear fission also produces a huge amount of heat energy, which is called nuclear energy.

Nuclear power

In a nuclear power station, the energy from nuclear fission is turned into electrical energy for use in factories, offices and homes. The reaction happens in a chamber called a nuclear reactor. Inside the reactor, a chain reaction happens but its speed is carefully controlled. The reaction produces a staggering amount of energy – just one gram of uranium fuel creates enough energy to run a light bulb continuously for 20 years!

Sellafield Nuclear Power Station in the UK. The reactor is inside the domed building in the centre.

Nuclear waste

Nuclear energy seems to be a good alternative to burning **fossil fuels** for producing energy, but it does create problems. The used fuel from nuclear power stations stays **radioactive** for thousands of years, so it has to be buried in concrete bunkers deep underground. Radioactive chemicals have also leaked from chemical plants into the seas and the **atmosphere**, where **radiation** from it may harm wildlife and people.

Nuclear fusion

Nuclear fusion is the opposite of nuclear fission. It is a nuclear reaction in which two nuclei join together to form a larger nucleus. Like fission, fusion releases huge amounts of energy. It is nuclear fusion that happens inside the Sun.

Accident at Chernobyl

The worst accident in the history of nuclear power happened at the Chernobyl nuclear power station in the Ukraine in 1986. The station's operators made several mistakes which allowed the reactor to run out of control, and 32 people were killed in the explosions and fires that followed. The radioactive substances that leaked from the reactor were carried across Europe by the wind, and people and animals later died from radiation sickness. Thousands more may die in the future because radiation levels in the area are still very high.

The periodic table

The periodic table is a chart of all the known **elements**. The elements are arranged in order of their atomic numbers, but in rows, so that elements with similar **properties** are underneath each other. The periodic table gets its name from the fact that the properties the elements have repeat themselves every few elements, or periodically. The position of an element in the periodic table gives an idea of what its properties are likely to be.

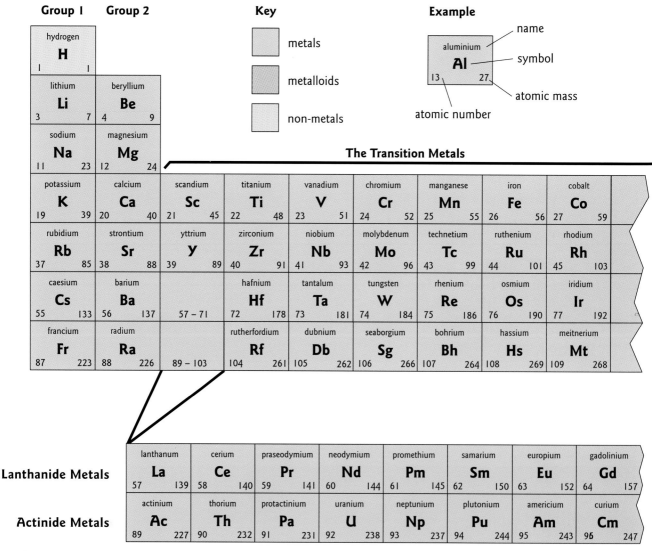

Groups and periods

The vertical columns of elements are called groups. The horizontal rows of elements are called periods. Some groups have special names:

Group 1: Alkali **metals**
Group 2: Alkaline earth metals
Group 7: Halogens
Group 0: Noble gases

The table is divided into two main sections, the metals and **non-metals**. Between the two are elements that have some properties of metals and some of non-metals. They are called semi-metals or **metalloids**.

Group 3	Group 4	Group 5	Group 6	Group 7	Group 0
					helium **He** 2 · 4
boron **B** 5 · 11	carbon **C** 6 · 12	nitrogen **N** 7 · 14	oxygen **O** 8 · 16	fluorine **F** 9 · 19	neon **Ne** 10 · 20
aluminium **Al** 13 · 27	silicon **Si** 14 · 28	phosphorus **P** 15 · 31	sulfur **S** 16 · 32	chlorine **Cl** 17 · 35	argon **Ar** 18 · 40
gallium **Ga** 31 · 70	germanium **Ge** 32 · 73	arsenic **As** 33 · 75	selenium **Se** 34 · 79	bromine **Br** 35 · 80	krypton **Kr** 36 · 84
indium **In** 49 · 115	tin **Sn** 50 · 119	antimony **Sb** 51 · 122	tellurium **Te** 52 · 128	iodine **I** 53 · 127	xenon **Xe** 54 · 131
thallium **Tl** 81 · 204	lead **Pb** 82 · 207	bismuth **Bi** 83 · 209	polonium **Po** 84 · 209	astatine **At** 85 · 210	radon **Rn** 86 · 222

(Left portion of lower rows:)

nickel **Ni** 28 · 59	copper **Cu** 29 · 64	zinc **Zn** 30 · 65
palladium **Pd** 46 · 106	silver **Ag** 47 · 108	cadmium **Cd** 48 · 112
platinum **Pt** 78 · 195	gold **Au** 79 · 197	mercury **Hg** 80 · 201
ununnilium **Uun** 110 · 271	unununium **Uuu** 111 · 272	ununbium **Uub** 112 · 285

ununquadium **Uuq** 114 · 289

terbium **Tb** 65 · 159	dysprosium **Dy** 66 · 163	holmium **Ho** 67 · 165	erbium **Er** 68 · 167	thulium **Tm** 69 · 169	ytterbium **Yb** 70 · 173	lutetium **Lu** 71 · 175
berkelium **Bk** 97 · 247	californium **Cf** 98 · 251	einsteinium **Es** 99 · 252	fermium **Fm** 100 · 257	mendelevium **Md** 101 · 258	nobelium **No** 102 · 259	lawrencium **Lr** 103 · 262

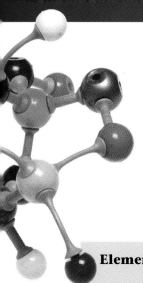

Common elements

Here is a table of the most common **elements** from the periodic table that you may come across at home or in the laboratory. The table gives the atomic mass (the total number of **protons** and **neutrons** in the **nucleus** of an **atom** of the element), indicates whether it is a solid, liquid or gas at room temperature, and how the atoms join together in a piece of the element.

Element	Symbol	Atomic mass	State at room temperature	Structure	Formula
hydrogen	H	1	gas	molecules	H_2
helium	He	4	gas	single atoms	He
lithium	Li	7	solid	metallic	
carbon	C	12	solid	giant molecules	
nitrogen	N	14	gas	molecules	N_2
oxygen	O	16	gas	molecules	O_2
fluorine	F	19	gas	molecules	F_2
neon	Ne	20	gas	single atoms	Ne
sodium	Na	23	solid	metallic	
magnesium	Mg	24	solid	metallic	
aluminium	Al	27	solid	metallic	
silicon	Si	28	solid	giant molecules	
phosphorus	P	31	solid	molecules	P_4
sulfur	S	32	solid	molecules	S_8
chlorine	Cl	35	gas	molecules	Cl_2
argon	Ar	40	gas	single atoms	Ar
potassium	K	39	solid	metallic	
calcium	Ca	40	solid	metallic	
iron	Fe	56	solid	metallic	
copper	Cu	64	solid	metallic	
zinc	Zn	65	solid	metallic	
bromine	Br	80	liquid	molecules	Br_2
silver	Ag	108	solid	metallic	
tin	Sn	119	solid	metallic	
iodine	I	127	solid	molecules	I_2
gold	Au	197	solid	metallic	
mercury	Hg	201	liquid	metallic	
lead	Pb	207	solid	metallic	

Common compounds

Here is a table of some common **compounds**, made up of two or more elements, that you may come across at home or in the laboratory. The middle column tells you what the **particles** of the compound are like.

Compound	Structure	Formula
Gases		
carbon dioxide	molecules	CO_2
carbon monoxide	molecules	CO
nitrogen dioxide	molecules	NO_2
methane	molecules	CH_4
Liquids and solutions		
water	molecules	H_2O
hydrochloric acid	ions in solution	HCl
sulfuric acid	ions in solution	H_2SO_4
nitric acid	ions in solution	HNO_3
sodium hydroxide	ions in solution	$NaOH$
Solids		
sodium chloride	ionic	$NaCl$
magnesium oxide	ionic	MgO
calcium carbonate	ionic	$CaCO_3$
copper sulfate	ionic	$CuSO_4$

Glossary of technical terms

atmosphere thick blanket of air that surrounds the Earth

atom extremely tiny particle of matter. An atom is the smallest particle of an element that can exist. All substances are made up of atoms.

atomic theory theory that all substances are made up of a limited number of types of atom combined together in different ways

boiling point temperature at which a substance changes state from liquid to gas

chain reaction series of nuclear reactions in which the particles emitted from one nucleus set off a reaction in another nucleus

charge electricity on an object, such as an atom or electron

chemical bond join between two atoms, ions or molecules

chemical formulae collection of symbols and numbers that represents an element or compound. It shows what elements are in a compound and the ratio of the numbers of atoms of each element.

compound substance that contains two or more different elements joined together by chemical bonds

condense turn from a gas to a liquid

conduct to let electricity or heat pass through a substance, called a conductor

covalent bond chemical bond formed when two atoms share one or more electrons

decay when the nucleus of an atom gradually becomes smaller and lighter as particles are ejected from it in nuclear reactions

diffusion random movement of the particles through a liquid or a gas

DNA very complex chemical in every living cell that carries the genetic information for the animal or plant

electron extremely tiny particle that is part of an atom. Electrons move around the nucleus of an atom.

element substance that contains just one type of atom. Elements are the simplest substances that exist.

fossil fuel natural fuel such as coal or gas, formed over thousands of years from the remains of living things

gene section of DNA which carries the code for making a protein. Genes are passed from one generation to the next.

genetic information information contained in genes as a complex chemical code. It controls how living cells are made and what they do.

ion type of particle. An ion is an atom that has lost or gained one or more electrons, giving it an overall positive or negative charge.

ionic bond chemical bond between two ions with opposite charges that attract each other

ionic compound compound made up of ions of two different elements

matter stuff that everything in the Universe is made from. There are three states of matter, and they are: solids, liquids and gases.

melting point temperature at which a substance changes state from solid to liquid as it warms

metal any element in the periodic table that is shiny, and that conducts electricity and heat well. Most metals are also hard.

metalloid element that cannot be classed as a metal or a non-metal. It has some of the properties of a metal and some of the properties of a non-metal.

mixture substance made up of two or more elements or compounds that are not joined together by chemical bonds

molecule type of particle. A molecule is made up of two or more atoms joined together by chemical bonds. The atoms can be of the same element or different elements.

neutron one of the particles that makes up the nucleus of an atom

non-metal any element in the periodic table that is not a metal. Most non-metals are gases.

nuclear fission nuclear reaction in which the nucleus of an atom splits into two parts

nucleus (nuclei) central part of an atom, made up of protons and neutrons

organic compound compounds found in living things, or in the remains of living things

particle small piece of a substance, such as an atom, ion or molecule

polymer compound that has molecules made up of lots of small molecules that are all the same, joined together in a long chain

properties characteristics of a substance, such as its strength, melting point and density

proton one of the particles that makes up the nucleus of an atom

radiation rays, such as light and heat, or streams of particles. Exposure to large amounts of radiation can be extremely harmful to people, animals and the environment.

radioactive describes a substance that gives off radiation

shells layers of electrons around the nucleus of an atom

solution substance made when a solid, gas or liquid dissolves in a liquid. The substance that dissolves is called the solute and the liquid it dissolves in is called the solvent.

sub-atomic particle particle that is part of an atom. Protons, neutrons and electrons are sub-atomic particles.

symbol single letter or two letters used to represent an element in chemical formulae and equations

theories ideas about how something, for example science, works

X-ray form of radiation that passes through flesh but is stopped by bones

Further reading

Chemical Chaos (Horrible Science)
Nick Arnold, Tony de Saulles, Scholastic Hippo, 1997

Chemicals in Action
Ann Fullick, Heinemann Library, 1999

Co-ordinated Science, Chemistry Foundation
Andy Bethell, John Dexter, Mike Griffths, Heinemann, 2001

The Dorling Kindersley Science Encyclopedia
Dorling Kindersley, 1993

How Science Works
Judith Hann, Dorling Kindersley, 1991

The Usborne Illustrated Dictionary of Chemistry
Jane Wertheim, Chris Oxlade and Dr. John Waterhouse
Usborne, 1987

Useful websites

http://www.heinemannexplore.com
An exciting new online resource for school libraries and classrooms containing articles, investigations, biographies and activities related to all areas of the science curriculum.

http://www.creative-chemistry.org.uk
An interactive chemistry site including fun practical activities, worksheets, quizzes, puzzles and more! With links to many more useful and interesting sites including:

http://www.bbc.co.uk/science
Loads of information on all areas of science. Includes news, activities, games and quizzes.

http://www.chemicool.com
All you ever needed to know about the elements – and more!

http://www.webelements.com/webelements/scholar
The Periodic table – online! Discover more about all the elements and their properties.

http://particleadventure.org
An interactive site, explaining the fundamentals of matter and forces!

Disclaimer
All the Internet addresses (URLs) given in this book were valid at the time of going to press. However, due to the dynamic nature of the Internet, some addresses may have changed, or sites may have ceased to exist since publication. While the author and publishers regret any inconvenience this may cause readers, no responsibility for any such changes can be accepted by either the author or the publishers.

Index

Titles in the *Chemicals in Action* series include:

Hardback   0 431 13603 3

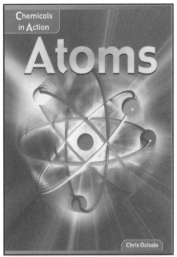

Hardback   0 431 13600 9

Hardback   0 431 13602 5

Hardback   0 431 13605 X

Hardback   0 431 13601 7

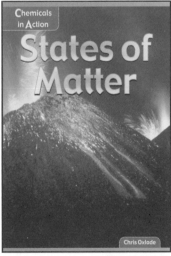

Hardback   0 431 13604 1

Find out about the other titles in this series on our website www.heinemann.co.uk/library